Favorite MEXICAN Recipes

JUDITH W. TOWLE

PELICAN PUBLISHING COMPANY

GRETNA   1978

Library of Congress Cataloging in Publication Data

Main entry under title:
 Favorite Mexican recipes.

 Includes index.
 1. Cookery, Mexican. I. Towle, Judith W.
TX716.M4F39   641.5'972   77-24145
ISBN 0-88289-157-X

Manufactured in the United States of America
Published by Pelican Publishing Company, Inc.
630 Burmaster Street, Gretna, Louisiana 70053

Cover design by Carol Edwards
Drawings by Judith W. Towle

Preface

I was born and raised in New Orleans but have lived in Mexico since 1958. Because my husband was born here, I developed an interest in Mexican food. These recipes have been collected from generous friends who have taught me traditional dishes commonly eaten in their homes.

Mexican food is a mixture of cultures . . . Originally Indian with Spanish, the French domination helps to enhance the repertoire; American, Italian, and German families have also contributed to the country and its cuisine.

This book originated as a Christmas present for family and friends who asked me to send them recipes for authentic Mexican food. With them in mind, I have tried to make explanations simple and have included an inexpensive shopping list to buy at supermarkets or Mexican food stores. When it is possible to substitute, reference is made.

All recipes are for six to eight servings unless otherwise specified.

Mexican food is easy to prepare, economical, and delicous! I hope you will agree!!

Special thanks to my family for trying all my experiments with a smile and to all the friends who have helped.

SHOPPING LIST

ACHIOTE — A concentrate of spices from Yucatan used for making sauces.

ADOBO — A sauce of spices and peppers. May be bought prepared.

CAJETA — A sweet milk product. Buy in jars.

CHILE ANCHO — A type of dried pepper.

CHILE CHIPOTLE EN ADOBO — Peppers prepared in Adobo Sauce and bought in cans.

CHILES CHIPOTLES EN VINAGRE — Same as above but pickled.

CHILES JALAPEÑOS — Pickled peppers. Buy in jars or cans.

CHILE PASILLA — A type of dried pepper.

CHILE PIQUIN — Small hot red peppers. Use like Cayenne Pepper.

CHILE POLBANOS — Large dark green and shiny. Buy fresh or canned.

CHILES SERRANOS (green chiles) — Most common type of fresh peppers, small dark green and shiny. Use fresh or canned.

JAMAICA — Small dried red flowers used for making a beverage.

MOLE — A sauce made of spices, peppers and chocolate. May be bought prepared.

NOPALES — Cactus leaves. Buy in cans or fresh.

PILONCILLO — Dark pressed sugar cones. Use for syrup (instead of brown sugar) with equal amounts of water.

TAMALE FLOUR — Comes packaged. I prefer "Tamale Harina" or "Mary Baker Tamale Mix."

TORTILLAS — Flat thin pancakes made out of corn or flour. Buy canned or frozen.

HERBS AND SUBSTITUTIONS

Do not use the same amount of dried herbs as fresh. In most cases 1 tsp. dried herbs equal 3 tsp. (1 Tbs.) fresh herbs.

¼ cup almonds . . . . .1 handful
1 cup consomme . . . . .1 cup water with 1 or 2 beef or chicken cubes
1 clove garlic . . . . .1/8 garlic powder
1 lemon peel grated . . . . .1 Tbs. grated lemon peel
1 orange peel grated . . . . .1 Tbs. grated orange peel
2 tsp. orange extract . . . . .1 tsp. grated orange peel
1 large onion, chopped . . . . .1 cup
1 large tomato, chopped . . . . .1 cup
1 large tomato . . . . .¼ cup canned tomato puree

Sauces

ADOBO SAUCE

This sauce is prepared. Then pork, chicken, or beef is simmered in it (either on top of the stove or baked) until tender.
About 2 cups.

6 chiles anchos
½ cup white vinegar
3 whole black peppers
1 stick cinnamon
 (consomee)

1 clove garlic
¼ onion
½ tsp. salt
2 Tbs. cooking oil

Boil chiles anchos with water and vinegar 10 minutes or until soft. Grind them in blender with rest of ingredients; then fry in hot oil for 5 minutes. Consomee may be added if sauce is too spicy.

ADOBO SAUCE WITH CONCENTRATE

2 Tbs. adobo paste
1 cup consomee

(1 Tbs. vinegar)

Dissolve paste in liquid. Or prepare a drier mixture and spread on meat or fowl before frying or baking.

ALMOND SAUCE

For tongue, chicken, or pork:

4 Tbs. cooking oil
¼ cup almonds (unpeeled)
1 onion, sliced
2 cloves garlic

½ slice white bread
1¼ cups consomee
2-3 tomatoes, chopped
salt and pepper

Saute in 2 Tbs. of oil almonds, onion, garlic, and bread (until onion is limp); add tomatoes and cook down until mushy. Grind in blender with consomee, then strain. Fry again in rest of oil and season to taste with salt and pepper.

GREEN TOMATO SAUCE

Served as a sauce or used as a base for meat and vegetables.

½ lb. Mexican green tomatoes   2 Tbs. parsley
½ cup water   1 Tbs. fresh corriander
¼ onion   ½ tsp. salt
2 cloves garlic   2 Tbs. cooking oil
1 green chile serrano

Heat a large frying pan with oil. Remove membrane covering green tomatoes and wash. Grind them in blender with rest of ingredients and add to hot oil. Cook down until thick.

Makes about 2 cups.

GUACAMOLE/BLENDER

To accompany meats, chicken, turkey, or anything served with tortillas.

2 large avocados peeled   ¼ tsp. salt
1 tsp. onion chopped   Milk

Grind avocado, onion, and salt with enough milk in blender to make smooth. Serve at room temperature or chilled.

GUACAMOLE/TRADITIONAL

Old time cooks serve "guacamole" with the seeds in, so that the sauce does not turn brown. For the same results: peel avocados, then run under cold tap water.

2 large ripe avocados, peeled   1 Tbs. fresh corriander
   and chopped   1 green chile serrano
3 Tbs. parsley, chopped   ¼ tsp. salt
¼ onion chopped fine   ½ cup chopped tomato

Mix or mash everything together. Serve at room temperature or chilled.

MOLE SAUCE

Mole is a sauce made with various kinds of peppers, spices, and chocolate.

It is the traditional sauce used on all special occasions.

Since its preparation is very elaborate and time consuming, modern households use pre-prepared concentrate bought at Mexican food stores.

Serve with Tacos and Enchiladas or use for simmering meat or fowl.

2 Tbs. Mole Concentrate   1 cup consomee

Mix Mole with consomee and heat.

NUT SAUCE

This is used cold for "Chiles en Nogada" and hot over chicken. When heating do not boil.

¾ cup pecans (or walnuts)   ¼ cup milk
½ cup thick cream   ½ tsp. salt (or chicken concentrate)

Grind everything in blender. Makes 1½ cups.

NUT SAUCE WITH PÂTE

Use this hot or cold over boiled chicken breasts or spread on crackers.

1½ cups Nut Sauce   ¾ cup pâté

Mix sauce and paté.

9

PIMIENTO AND CREAM SAUCE

A pretty pink sauce that may be served hot or cold. It especially combines well with shrimps, pork, and cauliflower.

1 cup sweet cream   ¼-½ cup red pimientos (canned)
½ tsp. salt

Grind ingredients in blender until smooth. When using hot do not boil. For meats, vegetables, and shrimp.

RED CHILE SAUCE

To accompany meats, chicken, or anything served with tortillas.

2 large tomatoes, chopped   3 Tbs. onion, chopped fine
1 green chile serrano,   3 Tbs. parsley, chopped
   chopped fine   1 Tbs. fresh coriander, chopped
1 Tbs. vinegar   salt

Mix everything together. Serve at room temperature or chilled.

TOMATO SAUCE

This is used as a sauce or as a base for soups and meats.

3 Tbs. bacon grease (cooking oil,   3 large tomatoes (or ¾ cup canned
   or olive oil)   tomato puree)
½ cup water   ¼ large onion
1 clove garlic   (1 green chile serrano)
5 sprigs parsley   ½ tsp. salt
¼ tsp. pepper

Heat a large frying pan with bacon grease. Grind in blender the rest of the ingredients and strain into the pan. Cook until the tomato separates from the grease. Makes approximately 2 cups.

TOMATO AND CREAM SAUCE

For meats and vegetables.

2 Tbs. bacon grease
1 clove garlic, chopped
2 cups tomato, chopped (or ½
   cup canned tomato puree)

¼ cup onion, chopped
1 green chile serrano
3 Tbs. cream (sweet or sour)
3 Tbs. ham, chopped

Saute onion, garlic, and chile in bacon grease until limp. Add tomato and cook down until tomato and oil separate. To serve, add cream and ham.

TOMATO WITH JALAPEÑOS SAUCE

To accompany meats, fowl or anything served with tortillas.

2 cups tomato, chopped
½ cup onion, chopped
¼ tsp. salt

1-4 Tbs. canned chiles jalapeños,
   chopped

Combine all ingredients. Serve at room temperature or chilled.

WHITE SAUCE

For meats and vegetables.

2 Tbs. onion
2 Tbs. flour
1 cup consomee

2 Tbs. butter
1 cup milk
salt and pepper

Whiz all ingredients in blender. Thicken on low heat until the sauce has a velvety consistency. Serve hot.

11

SALSA BORRACHA (Drunkard Sauce)

Specially good with pork, chicken, and eggs.

6 chiles pasilla
1 clove garlic
1 cup pulque (or beer)
2 Tbs. onion, chopped
½ tsp. salt

½ cup water
2 Tbs. oil
1 green chile (serrano)
2 Tbs. cheese, grated

Cut chiles pasilla open and remove seeds and veins. Place them in water and boil until water is consumed.

Grind them with garlic, oil, pulque, and green chile in blender. Add onion, cheese, and salt to serve. Serve at room temperature.

Tortillas and How to Use Them

CORN TORTILLAS

This is the most well known type of tortilla. Recipes refer to this kind of tortilla for most Mexican food. When flour tortillas are used this is specified.

True tortilla dough is made by soaking corn in lime water over night, then grinding. Some households use a prepared corn meal called Minsa. Mix 2 cups Minsa with 1 cup flour and enough warm water to make pliable. Dough is then hand patted to form thin pancakes or placed between 2 sheets of plastic in a tortilla press, then cooked on a hot griddle.

Most households (including ours) buy tortillas that are prepared and sold by special venders.

Tortillas are always heated before eating or rolling. If they are old, run under tap water first. Heat on a griddle or dry frying pan, or for large amounts steam.

FLOUR TORTILLAS

These are eaten in northern Mexico and are very easy to make. Tacos made with these are called "burritos" (little donkies) and are never fried.

2 cups flour	½ tsp. salt
4 Tbs. vegetable shortening	

Mix flour, salt, and shortening. Add enough warm water to make a soft dough. Divide into balls the size of an egg and let rest 20 minutes. Roll out on a floured board as thin as possible. Cut around any 6 " canister top to make tortillas uniform in size. Cook on a hot griddle two minutes on each side and stack in a pretty napkin. Tortillas should be soft and pliable enough to roll into a "taco". They may be reheated again on hot griddle to serve.

CHILAQUILES OR BUDIN DE TORTILLA

Tortillas are quickly passed through hot oil. They are placed in an ovenproof dish in layers with meat, vegetables, sauce, and always ending with cheese. This is heated in a hot oven 20 minutes.

15

Good combinations using 18 tortillas and ½ cup grated cheese:

1)   2 cups tomato sauce (or green tomato sauce)
     1 cup chopped chicken (or pork)

2)   1½ cups Mole Sauce
     ½ cup sour cream
     1 cup chopped chicken (or pork)

3)   1 cup milk
     1 cup cream
     1 cup chopped chicken
     ½ cup cooked corn

ENCHILADAS

Tortillas are quickly passed through hot oil then drained.
To serve individually, place in the center of each tortilla cooked, chopped meat. Roll like a cigar, and pour sauce on top. To serve a large family or party, dip each tortilla in sauce, spread with cooked, chopped meat and roll. These are placed in a greased ovenproof dish and heated in a hot oven 20 minutes.
Either way, enchiladas are always served with cream, grated cheese, and onion rings on top.

Traditional enchiladas; quantities are for 18 tortillas and serve 6.

Enchiladas Rojas (Red)

2 cups chopped chicken   2 cups tomato sauce

Enchiladas Verdes (Green)

2 cups chopped chicken   2 cups green tomato sauce

Enchiladas de Mole

2 cups chopped chicken (or pork)   2 cups Mole Sauce

16

ENCHILADAS WITH CHILE ANCHO

These are worth a special trip to a Mexican food store to buy the 2 kinds of chiles.

3 chiles anchos
1 Tbs. vinegar
2 eggs
1 boiled chicken, chopped
salt, pepper, cooking oil
onion rings

2 chiles chipotles en adobo
1 Tbs. sugar
2-3 cloves garlic
25 tortillas
Swiss cheese

Soak chiles anchos an hour in warm water. Grind them in blender with chiles chipotles, vinegar, sugar, garlic, and eggs. Quickly pass tortillas through hot cooking oil, then dip in sauce. Roll with chicken inside and place in a greased ovenproof dish. Cover with any leftover sauce, onion rings, and grated cheese. Heat in a hot oven 20 minutes or until cheese melts.

ENFRIJOLADAS

2 cups beans (cooked) with
    their liquid
¼ onion
18 tortillas

1 large tomato (or ¼ cup canned
    tomato puree)
1 clove garlic
salt, cooking oil

Garnishes: grated cheese or cottage cheese, chopped onion, sweet or sour cream.

Pass tortillas quickly through hot oil. Drain and reserve. Leave 2 Tbs. oil in pan and add the following mixture: Grind in blender the rest of ingredients, adding more bean or plain water in order to have a runny mixture. Let cook down 10 minutes.

To serve, dip tortillas in the hot bean sauce and fold into fourths with a spatula, and pass the garnishes.

ENTOMATADAS

These are prepared and served in the same manner as Enfrijoladas. The fried tortillas are dipped in Tomato Sauce or Green Tomato Sauce instead of beans.

TACOS AND CREPES

A corn or flour tortilla is spread with filling and rolled like a cigar. The sauce or pickled chiles is always served separately.

1) Corn or flour tortillas are heated on a hot griddle and each person fills his own taco at the table.

2) Corn tortillas are filled and fried in the kitchen before serving. Tan for soft tortillas; brown for crisp tortillas.

Any filling used for tacos may be used for crepes. Spread filling in the center of each crepe, roll, then place in greased ovenproof dish in a hot oven 20 minutes. Serve with cream on top.
Specially good this way!

Suggested fillings:

1) Picadillo

2) Chicken in tomato sauce

3) Leftover Chicken Mole

4) Hardboiled eggs and green pimiento strips

CHICKEN TACOS

Everyone's favorite. The trick is to chop the chicken's skin with the meat.

18 tortillas

1 boiled chicken and skin diced (about 2 cups)

Place chicken in tortillas. Follow instructions for all tacos. If tacos are not to be fried, chicken meat should be warmed in consomee or butter. Serve with refried beans and any Mexican sauce.

TACOS SUDADOS (Steamed Tacos)

These are very good and are specially practical.

Fill tortillas with stuffing. Place "tacos" in a napkin and steam (I use an old baby bottle sterilizer) 20 minutes or until hot. Turn off heat. These will remain hot at least 30 minutes more if top is left on pot.

TOSTADAS

Fried tortillas that are dark brown and crisp.

1) They may be purchased pre-prepared.
2) Tortillas may be deep fried until dark brown and drained.
3) Tortillas may be spread with cooking oil on both sides, placed on a cookie sheet, and baked in a hot oven 30 minutes or until dark brown.

They are put together in the following order:

**refried beans
chopped lettuce
chopped cooked meat (chicken, fried chorizo, or pork sausage)
chopped onion
grated cheese or cottage cheese
sweet or sour cream
(chile sauce or pickled chiles are served separately)**

TOTOPOS

Tortillas are cut in fourths, forming triangles. These are fried until brown and crisp. They can be eaten plain with salt, dipped in Guacamole Sauce, or refried beans. Calculate one or two tortillas per person.

QUESADILLAS

Authentic quesadillas are made out of uncooked corn tortilla dough that is made into a flat pancake, filled folded, pinched together, and fried in deep fat. They can also be made with corn tortillas that are filled, folded in half, and either fried in cooking oil or heated on a hot griddle, and pressed down with a spatula or any flat pot top.

19

If flour tortillas are to be used, quesadillas are always heated on a griddle.

Common fillings:

1) any kind of cheese

2) mashed potatoes

3) ham and cheese

4) brains sauteed with onions

Snacks

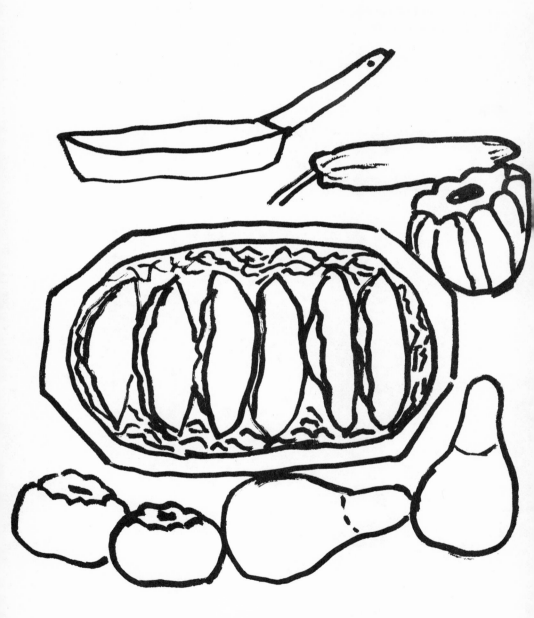

ANCHOVY SPREAD

Mash:

2 cans anchovies with capers   3 hard-boiled eggs
½ tsp. mustard

Spread on crackers.

FRESH HORS D'OEUVRES

Cucumbers-sliced lengthwise   Carrots-sliced lengthwise in strips
   in strips   Orange slices

Squeeze lemon on top, then sprinkle with salt, cayenne pepper, Tabasco sauce, or paprika.

EMPANADAS

These are "turnovers" made out of pie dough or puff paste rolled thin and cut in three inch circles. They are filled and folded in half. The sides are pinched, the top is painted with egg white and they are baked on a greased cookie sheet 30 minutes or until golden.

Common fillings:

1) any leftovers (meat or   2) tuna fish with thick cream sauce
   vegetables)   3) Picadillo with olives
4) stew   5) cheese
6) mole

Use about one Tbs. filling for each empanada.

FRENCH BREAD WITH BEANS AND CHEESE (Molletes)

French bread   Refried beans
Cheese   Any Mexican sauce or pickled
                                    chiles

Spread one inch slices of French bread with refried beans and place on top a small slice of cheese. Place under broiler until the cheese melts. Serve with any Mexican sauce.

GREEN ONIONS

10 to 12 green onions   2 Tbs. cooking oil
(Garnishes: sliced lemon and salt)

Leave the stems on the onions. Cook on a hot griddle with oil, turning continually until soft. Serve with garnishes.

MELTED CHEESE

4, 2" pieces chorizo (or pork   3 cups Swiss cheese, cubed
   sausage), mashed   Flour tortillas

Fry chorizo until golden in a small pretty skillet. Drain off any excess oil. Add cheese, lower heat, and cook until cheese is melted, (or bake in the oven 20 minutes). Serve with hot Flour tortillas.

For variations:

1)   Add strips of green pepper or chile poblano deveined
2)   Serve with tomato sauce

MEXICAN STEAK TARTAR

Quantities are for one cup meat. Serve with toast squares or crackers.

1 cup ground beef
2 Tbs. olive oil
½ tsp. Maggi Sauce
1/8 tsp. pepper

2 Tbs. lemon juice
½ tsp. Worcestershire Sauce
¼ tsp. salt
1 small green chile serrano chopped
(or a few drops Tabasco sauce)

Combine all ingredients and let sit 30 minutes before serving.

SHRIMP WITH SNOW

Grind onion with lemon juice in blender. Serve over boiled shrimp.

TORTAS

The Mexican equivalent to sandwiches. In Mexico one can buy "teleras" which are rolls specially made for this purpose. Any good French bread may be substituted and the same results are obtained. All tortas may be served at room temperature or heated on a hot griddle with enough cooking oil so that they won't stick. Serve with pickled chiles.

CHICKEN TORTAS

For making lots of "tortas" it is much easier to make a recipe of Guacamole Sauce instead of plain avocado.

1 loaf French bread
sliced chicken (ham, roasted
   pork, roasted turkey)
1 slice Swiss cheese

refried beans
chopped lettuce
sliced tomato
sliced avocado

Cut French bread in four inch lengths, then split lengthwise. Spread top with refried beans, place the rest of the ingredients on bottom, then close. Serve with pickled chiles.

25

PEPITOS

1 loaf French bread
mustard
Guacamole Sauce (or sliced
    avocado)

small thin steaks
refried beans
salt and pepper

Cut French bread in four inch lengths, then split lengthwise. Sprinkle steaks with salt and pepper and pan fry. Assemble in the following way from bottom in this order: mustard, steak; on top: mustard, refried beans, guacamole, and close. These are superior when heated.

Soups

ALPHABET SOUP

Children always like this soup.

3½ oz. (¾ cup) alphabet letters
1 tomato (or ¼ cup canned
    tomato puree)
1 cup water
2 Tbs. parsley, chopped

2 Tbs. cooking oil
¼ onion
1 clove garlic
5 cups consomme

Fry letters in oil until golden. Grind tomato, onion, garlic, and water in blender. Strain and add to letters. Add consomme and parsley and boil covered until the letters are soft. About 30 minutes.

HOT AVOCADO SOUP

4 tortillas
6 cups consomme
2 large avocados, peeled

cooking oil
2 tomatoes (or ½ cup tomato puree)

Cut tortillas in thin strips and fry until dark brown and crisp. Drain and reserve. Grind tomatoes with 1 cup consomme and strain. Add this to the rest of the consomme and boil 25 minutes. To serve: mash avocados in soup tureen and pour over hot soup. Pass the tortilla strips for garnish.

ARTICHOKE SOUP

5 artichokes
½ tsp. salt
1 beef cube
1/8 tsp. nutmeg
1 Tbs. cornstarch

water
1½ cups milk (or 1 cup milk, ½ cup
    cream)
¼ tsp. pepper

Cover artichokes with water, add salt, and cook until tender. Separate hearts, remove thistle, slice, and reserve, (if you have time, scrape leaves with a spoon and add this to soup).

Grind the leaves of four artichokes (throw the other away) in blender with the water they were cooked in, strain into a soup pot, add milk, nutmeg, pepper, beef cube, and sliced hearts. Simmer 20 minutes. If you wish to thicken soup, mix cornstarch in one-fourth cup of water, add to soup and simmer five minutes more.

29

COLD AVOCADO SOUP

2 cups Leek and Potato Soup   1 cup avocado pulp
3 cups consomme, well seasoned   extra avocado slices

Grind soup, avocado pulp, and consomme in blender until smooth. (This should have the consistency of Vichyssoise; if thick add more consomme.)

Serve avocado slices floating on top.

BACON AND TOMATO SOUP

2 tomatoes (or ½ cup canned   6 cups water
    tomato puree)   2 leeks, sliced
2 potatoes, peeled and chopped   6 slices bacon, diced
2 Tbs. parsley, chopped   2 chicken cubes
salt and pepper

Place all the ingredients in a pot and simmer until the potatoes are soft. About one hour.

BEAN SOUP

2 cups cooked beans and their   1 large tomato
    liquid   ¼ onion
1 clove garlic   4 cups consomme (or chicken cubes
2 Tbs. cooking oil   and water)
Salt to taste

Garnishes: fried tortilla strips, chopped cheese.

Grind beans, tomato, onion, and garlic in blender. Strain and add to hot oil. Add consomme and cook on low heat 30 mintues. Add salt to taste and serve with garnishes.

CORN CHOWDER

4 ears corn, degrained
¼ cup grated cheese
1 cup milk

3 potaotes, peeled and cubed
5 cups consomme
salt, pepper, freshly ground

Simmer all ingredients on a low flame until corn is cooked. About one hour. Add pepper to serve.

CREAM SOUPS

Great!
Cook any green vegetable in the least amount of water possible. Grind in the blender with enough of the vegetable water to make a loose puree. Strain, add enough milk to give a soup consistency. Season with beef or chicken cubes and pepper.
Cook on a low flame 20 minutes.

Variations:

Cream of Spinach

Add nutmeg and croutons

Cream of Corn

Add cubed Swiss cheese, chopped pimentos, or green peppers

Cream of Cauliflower

Add lots of freshly ground pepper

Cream of Tomato

Add fried pieces of chorizo, pork sausages, or fried tortilla strips

Cream of Potato

Add chopped watercress

31

CREAM OF PECAN

1½ cups pecans
1 cube beef bouillon
1 Tbs. onion chopped fine
½ cup tomato puree
½ cup cream
salt, pepper, and nutmeg

6 cups consomme
½ cup butter
1 clove garlic, mashed
1 Tbs. cornstarch
1 egg yolk

Grind pecans with consomme in blender. Saute onion and garlic in butter until limp, add nut mixture and cornstarch that has been wet with a little water. Cook ½ hour. To serve: beat egg yolk with cream; add to hot soup.

CHICKEN CONSOMME

Easy and never fails!

1 chicken
2 stalks celery and leaves
5 sprigs parsley
¼ tsp. pepper

1 onion, quartered
2 carrots, cut lengthwise
½ tsp. salt
2 chicken cubes (optional)

Place all of the ingredients in a pot and barely cover with water. Boil until chicken is tender. (About one hour.) Remove meat from bones and return them to pot and boil 20 minutes more.

VARIATIONS FOR CONSOMME

When ready to serve consomme add one of the following:

1) Beat raw eggs into hot soup with a fork
2) Chopped tomato, onion, avocado
3) Any chile sauce
4) Rice
5) Strips of crepes
6) Hot cake mix that has been cooked, dribbled on a hot griddle
7) Tortilla strips, fried
8) Leftover vegetables
9) Chopped ham, cooked chicken, and cooked steak
10) Shredded chicken, slices of avocado, slices of Swiss cheese, 3 Tbs. sweet cream

FISH SOUP

2 lbs. fish, chopped (including
    head and tail)
¼ tsp. pepper
2 cups tomato sauce
sweet pickles, chopped fine

1 bay leaf
½ tsp. salt
2 potatoes, cubed
chiles jalapenos
water

Cover fish with water, add bay leaf, salt and pepper, and boil 30 minutes or until done—strain fish stock and add with potatoes to tomato sauce. Cook until potatoes are done. To serve: remove bones from fish and add to soup. Pass chiles and pickles on a separate plate.

GASPACHO

This is how it is done in Mexico.

2 lbs. ripe tomatoes (about 8
    large)
½ tsp. salt
½ cup olive oil

2 slices French bread or 2 slices
    regular white bread
¼ cup red wine vinegar
4 drops Tabasco Sauce

Garnishes: cucumber, sliced thin; parsley, chopped; avocado, sliced

Grind tomatoes with bread in blender. Refrigerate at least 2 hours, then grind again. Strain. Place in soup tureen and season with vinegar, oil, salt, and Tabasco. Garnishes may be served floating in soup or separately.

LEEK AND POTATO SOUP

With the leftovers of this soup I make Vichyssoise. Blend them with cream or milk, add chicken cubes, and chopped chives.

3 large potatoes, peeled,
    and cubed
6 cups consomme

2 leeks, thinly sliced
3 Tbs. parsley, chopped

Cook everything together until potatoes are soft. About 30 minutes.

MUSHROOM SOUP

Serve this to gourmet friends.

6 cups consomme
2 egg yolks
½ cup sour cream
salt and pepper

½ lb. fresh mushrooms, washed
(about 4 cups)
1 tsp. dry sherry

Boil mushrooms in consomme until tender. (About 30 minutes.) Grind in blender. To serve: beat yolks with sour cream and add to hot soup. Add sherry and season with salt and pepper.

NOODLE SOUP

This soup is so good, one never tires of it. I always make 7 oz. pasta, since the leftovers, when heated, strained, and served with parmesan cheese and sweet cream on top take on a different flavor that is even better than the first day.

Vermicelli noodles are thin like thread, like those used in Campbell's Chicken and Noodle Soup.

5 Tbs. cooking oil
2 tomatoes (or ½ cup canned nato tomato puree)
1 clove garlic
2 Tbs. chopped parsley
1 potato, chopped (optional)

7 oz. vermicelli noodles (1 package)
1 cup water
¼ onion
7 cups consomme
1 carrot, chopped (optional)

Break then fry noodles in hot cooking oil until golden. Strain noodles and reserve. Leave 2 Tbs. oil in pot, and strained tomatoes, onion, and garlic which have been ground in blender. Add the rest of the ingredients and cook covered until pasta is soft. About 30 minutes.

POZOLE

This is a meal in itself, especially nice on cold days.

3 cups canned hominy, drained
1 onion
½ tsp. salt

1 lb. pork shoulder, in small cubes
water
¼ tsp. pepper

34

Garnishes: chopped onion and cabbage, sliced radishes, oregano, lemon
slices

Cover pork and onion with water, add salt and pepper, and cook
one hour or until well done. Add cooked hominy and cook ten minutes
more. Serve with garnishes.

POZOLE (RED)

Add half the following to Pozole at the same time as hominy;
cook ten minutes. Serve the rest of sauce with garnishes.

1 chile ancho
1 large clove garlic
1 slice onion
1 whole clove
1 large tomato, parboiled
     5 minutes

1 chile pasilla
1 cup broth from Pozole
2 Tbs. bacon grease (or oil)
1 whole black pepper

Toast chiles on a hot griddle turning over until bubbles form on
skin; toast garlic on griddle until soft.
Boil toasted chiles, garlic, and onion in water until soft. Throw
away chile water; grind chile with broth from pozole in blender.
Heat bacon grease and add chile mixture, clove, and black pepper.
Grind tomato in blender, strain, and add to sauce. Cook down
until thick.

SHRIMP BROTH

This is commonly served for hangovers in bars and after parties at
sunrise.

1 lb. dried shrimp (soaked over-
    night then peeled)
2 cloves garlic
2 Tbs. olive oil
salt and pepper

5 cups water
1 onion
2 tomatoes (or ½ cup canned
    tomato puree)
Tabasco Sauce or chiles chipotles
    en adobo

Boil shrimp in water one hour or until soft.

Grind onion, garlic, and tomato with one-half cup shrimp water.

Strain. In a frying pan heat olive oil, add tomato mixture, and cook until tomato separates from oil. Add this to shrimp (and water) and simmer 30 minutes. Season to taste with salt, pepper, Tabasco Sauce, or chiles chipotles.

TORTILLA SOUP

8 tortillas, cut in thin strips
3 tomatoes (¾ cup canned
 tomato puree)
1 clove garlic
½ tsp. salt
4 to 6 cups consomme

3 Tbs. cooking oil
½ cup water
¼ onion
5 sprigs parsley
½ tsp. pepper

Fry tortillas in hot oil until brown and crisp. Drain and reserve. Leave 3 Tbs. cooking oil in pot and add tomatoes, water, onion, garlic, parsley, salt, and pepper that have been ground in blender, then strained. Add consomme and boil 30 minutes.

To serve: pour hot soup over tortillas.

Pastas, Rice, and Eggs

ARRÓZ CON POLLO (Rice with Chicken)

I prefer "never fail" parboiled rice for this. For regular rice: brown chicken then follow the recipe for white rice using consomme instead of water.

1 chicken, cut in serving pieces
1 cup parboiled rice
½ cup chopped onion
1 clove garlic
salt and pepper

4 Tbs. olive oil
consomme (my brand calls for 4
    cups liquid for 1 cup rice)
1 Tbs. canned tomato puree

Season chicken with salt and pepper and brown on both sides in olive oil with onion and garlic. Add tomato puree and cook 1 minute. Add rice, mix with chicken, and add consomme. Turn heat to low, cover, and cook 30 minutes or until the chicken is tender and rice is fluffy.

PAELLA (Rice with Meat and Seafood)

A meal in itself, this is spectacular for company. In families of Spanish descent this is used for parties. The guests are invited early to watch the host prepare this on a special wood fire in the garden. The ingredients are the same whether inside or outside.

If possible use a paella pan: a shallow frying pan with handles on both sides. This is used for both preparation and serving.

Olive oil
½ lb. spare ribs (or pork
    shoulder, cubed)
1 cup onion, chopped fine
1 cup tomatoes, chopped (or ¼
    cup canned tomato puree)
8 cups consomme boiled with
    ½ tsp. saffron
2/3 cup red pimientos (1 small
    can) cut in strips
½ cup cooked carrots (optional)

½ chicken, cut in serving pieces
4 crabs, cleaned and broken in half,
    and 16 shrimps
2 cloves garlic
2 cups parboiled rice (my brand
    calls for 4 cups liquid for each
    cup of rice)
6 small artichokes, parboiled and
    cut in half
½ cup cook peas (optional)
½ cup cooked snap beans (optional)

Coat paella pan with olive oil and heat. Sprinkle meat with salt and pepper and brown on one side. When ready to turn over add seafood, onion, and garlic and cook until everything is almost done. Add

39

tomato and fry 2 minutes more. Add rice, consomme, and artichokes. Lower heat and cover with a large pot top or kitchen towels that have been dampened and wrung out. Cook until rice if fluffy (20-25 minutes) and decorate with pimiento strips (and cooked vegetables) to serve.

RED AND WHITE RICE GARNISHES

1. Fried banana slices
2. Hard boiled egg, chopped
3. Chopped chicken livers and gizzards, sauteed
4. Chorizo, fried and chopped
5. Fried eggs
6. Sliced avocado
7. Small tacos
8. Lots of chopped parsley
9. Thin strips of chile poblano or green pepper
10. Small cooked artichokes
11. Any Mexican sauce or pickled chiles
12. Any kind of cooked beans

RED RICE

1 cup rice
½ onion
1 tomato (or ¼ cup canned
    tomato puree)
½ cup cooked carrots, peas,
    potatoes (optional)

½ cup cooking oil
1 clove garlic
2¼ cups water
½ tsp. salt (or 1 beef cube)

Soak rice in hot water 15 minutes. Rinse in a strainer with cold tap water until the water is no longer cloudy. Drain well. In a large pan, fry rice until it is almost golden. Drain off excess oil. Grind tomatoes with onion, garlic, and water. Strain, add to rice and cooked vegetables. Cover and turn the heat to low. Cook until fluffy. If you must stir, use a fork.

WHITE RICE

Exactly enough for 6.

1 cup rice
½ onion, chopped
½ tsp. salt
2½ cups water
1 Tbs. lemon juice (this keeps the
    rice white)

½ cup cooking oil
1 clove garlic
½ cup cooked carrots, peas, and
    potatoes (optional)

Soak rice in hot water 15 minutes. Rinse in a strainer with cold tap water until the water is no longer cloudy. Drain well. In a large pan fry rice with onion and garlic until it is no longer transparent. Strain off oil. Add water, vegetables, salt, and lemon juice; cover. Turn heat to low and cook until the rice is fluffy. If you must stir, use a fork.

RICE WITH CREAM AND CHEESE

4 cups cooked white rice
½ cup sweet cream
½ tsp. salt
¼ tsp. pepper

1 cup Swiss cheese, grated
3 green peppers (or chiles poblanos,
    deveined) cut in strips

Make layers of rice, cheese, and pepper strips, ending with cheese. Pour cream seasoned with salt and pepper over the top and bake in a hot oven 20 minutes.

RICE RING

4 cups cooked white rice
1 can evaporated milk
¼ tsp. salt

3 green peppers (bell or poblanos,
    deveined)
2 hard boiled eggs, sliced thin

Grease a ring mold and press rice in tightly. Bake 20 minutes (to set) at 350 F.

Sauce: Grind peppers with evaporated milk, season with salt. Then strain and heat.

To serve: Invert molded rice on platter, pour sauce over and garnish with hard boiled egg slices.

FOR BETTER SPAGHETTI AND NOODLES

Using this Mexican method any pasta may be prepared early or refrigerated and it will not become mushy.

Cook spaghetti or noodles in boiling water to which you add salt, 1 Tbs. cooking oil, and ¼ tsp. black pepper. When it has reached the desired consistency rinse with cold tap water and drain. Then mix or prepare in desired way.

To heat pastas that have been refrigerated, place prepared oven-proof dish in a cold oven. Turn on heat to 500 F and calculate at least 30 minutes adding a little bit of water if necessary.

NOODLES WITH CREAM

4 cups broad noodles (or spaghetti), cooked
½ cup grated parmesan cheese

1 cup cream (sweet or sour)
4 Tbs. Maggi Sauce
pepper, freshly ground

Mix all of the ingredients saving a little cheese for the top. Heat in a hot oven 20 minutes or until sauce bubbles.

NOODLES WITH GARLIC

4 cups cooked broad noodles
¼ cup water
2-3 large cloves garlic, mashed

¼ cup butter, cut in pieces
¼ cup Maggi Sauce
1 cup grated cheese

Mix all of the ingredients in a greased ovenproof dish, reserving ½ cup cheese to sprinkle on top. Bake in a hot oven 20 minutes or until the cheese melts.

PASTAS WITH HAM AND CREAM

4 cups cooked pasta (noodles, macaroni, spaghetti, etc.)
1 Tbs. Maggi Sauce
1 cup ham in cubes

1 cup sweet cream
1 cup grated cheese
salt and pepper to taste

Combine all ingredients reserving ½ cup cheese for top. Heat oven (500 F) and cook for 20 minutes.

42

RED SPAGHETTI

My favorite!

4 cups cooked spaghetti	2 cups tomato sauce
¼ cup sour (or sweet cream)	½ cup grated cheese

Mix spaghetti and tomato sauce in an ovenproof dish. Dab with sour cream and sprinkle cheese on top. Bake 20 minutes in a hot oven or until the cheese melts.

EGGS A LA MEXICANA
(Serves 2)

1 Tbs. bacon grease	2 Tbs. chopped onion
1 clove garlic	½ green chile serrano, chopped
½ cup chopped tomatoes	4 eggs, well beaten
salt	

Saute onion and garlic until limp in bacon grease; add tomato and chile; cook 2 minutes or until mushy; add eggs and salt to taste; cook until firm.

DROWNED EGGS

6 eggs   2 cups tomato sauce

Heat sauce to simmering point and carefully break eggs into it. Poach until firm. This is served by itself for breakfast or over white rice.

EGGS GUANAJUATO STYLE .

This dish is nice for Sunday night supper.

2 cups tomato sauce with 1 bay	12 eggs
leaf and ¼ tsp. oregano added	2 Tbs. cooking oil
salt and pepper	

Scramble eggs with salt and pepper and pour into a large pan with heated oil. Let sit open, like an omelet until almost firm. Remove from heat and cut in serving pieces. Pour over sauce and return to heat. While eggs finish cooking be sure the sauce penetrates the bottom of eggs as well.

EGGS RANCH STYLE

4 eggs
½ cup chopped onion
1 Tbs. cooking oil
1 green chile serrano, chopped

4 tortillas
1 clove garlic, chopped
2 cups chopped tomatoes
¼ tsp. salt

Fry onion, garlic, and chile in oil until limp. Add tomato and salt; cook until mushy. In another pan quickly pass tortillas in hot cooking oil, then drain. Fry eggs and place an egg on each tortilla and cover with sauce.

EGGS WITH CHORIZO

1 Tbs. cooking oil
4 eggs, well beaten
salt and pepper

2" length chorizo (or pork sausage), mashed

Fry chorizo in oil until brownish. Remove any extra oil and add eggs which have been beaten with salt and pepper to taste. Cook until firm.

EGGS YUCATAN SYTLE (Motuleños)

1 egg
1 Tbs. refried beans
1 Tbs. chopped ham
1 Tbs. grated cheese

1 tortilla
1 Tbs. cooked peas
2 to 3 Tbs. tomato sauce

Fry tortilla until dark brown, then drain (or use bought tostadas). Spread tortilla with refried beans and place on top the fried egg, peas, ham, tomato sauce, and cheese.

SCRAMBLED EGGS WITH BEANS

2 eggs, beaten
1 Tbs. oil
salt and pepper

2 Tbs. cooked beans (or refried beans)

Heat oil in frying pan. Add beans, then eggs. Season to taste with salt and pepper, cook until firm.

44

Meat, Fowl, and Fish

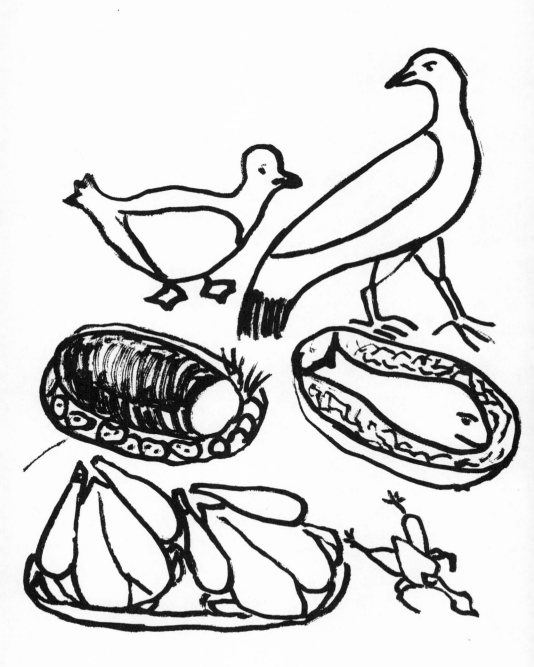

CHICKEN BREASTS WITH CHIPOTLE

7 chicken breasts, boiled and
  deboned
¼ tsp. salt

1 to 3 canned Chipotles en Adobo
1 cup sweet cream
½ cup Swiss cheese, grated

Place chicken breasts in a greased ovenproof dish. Grind chiles with cream in blender. Season with salt and pour over chicken. Sprinkle with cheese and heat 20 minutes in a hot oven or until cheese melts.

CHICKEN AND PEPPER CREPES

4 cups White Sauce
1 cup grated cheese
3 green peppers (or chile
  poblano fresh or canned,
  in stripes)

2 cups chicken, cooked and
  chopped
1 recipe crepes

Mix 2 cups of White Sauce with chicken. Place green peppers, then chicken in the center of each crepe. Roll and place in a greased ovenproof dish. Pour over the rest of the sauce and sprinkle cheese on top. Heat in a hot oven 20 minutes or until cheese melts.

COVERED CHICKEN

A traditional dish from Puebla. It is very easy to prepare and a good company dish. Serve with white rice.

1 chicken, cut in serving pieces
¼ cup chopped onion
½ cup green olives (optional)
salt and pepper
1 cup water

2 chopped tomatoes (2 cups)
¼ cup blanched almonds
2 Tbs. capers (optional)
butter

Sprinkle chicken with salt and pepper. Place it with the rest of the ingredients in a heavy skillet or dutch oven greased with butter. Cover and simmer, stirring once in a while until chicken is tender about 45 minutes. More water may be added if the chicken begins to stick.

CHICKEN MOLE

Classic for fiestas!

1 large chicken, cut in serving pieces	1 onion
½ tsp. salt	2 cloves garlic
¼ cup sesame seeds	Mole concentrate (2 Tbs. for each
tortillas	cup liquid)

Barely cover chicken with water. Add onion, garlic, and salt. Cook until tender. About 1 hour. Prepare Mole Sauce with consomme from chicken. Add chicken to this and simmer 30 minutes. To serve: brown sesame seeds in a dry frying pan and sprinkle over chicken. Have tortillas hot for making tacos.

GUERAS CHICKEN

This looks more complicated than it really is!

For Brown Sauce:

6 Tbs. butter	6 Tbs. flour
1 can beef consomme	1 can water
4 slices bacon	1 Tbs. carrots, chopped
1 Tbs. onion, grated	½ clove garlic
1 tsp. tomato paste	1 bouquet garnis (bay leaf, thyme,
1 Tbs. Bovril (beef extract)	with parsley on the outside)
salt and pepper	

Chicken:

1½ chicken cut in serving pieces	salt and pepper
½ cup butter	5 slices bacon
2 cups white wine	18 small white onions
18 mushrooms	18 olives with pimento

Make Brown Sauce first: Saute butter and flour until brown. Add consomme and water. In another pan fry bacon, carrots, and grated onion until limp and combine with the first part. Add garlic, tomato paste, bouquet garnis, Bovril, salt and pepper, and boil half an hour, then strain.

Chicken: Season chicken with salt and pepper, then fry in butter until almost done. Remove it from pan and fry bacon until crisp. Remove some of the grease and then return chicken, wine, onions, mushrooms, olives, and Brown Sauce. Cover and simmer 34 minutes. To thicken sauce add flour diluted in water and boil until thick.

RED OR GREEN CHICKEN

Try serving this with chopped avocado added to sauce. Sauce may be prepared in advance or prepared in the same pot as chicken after it has been browned.

2 Tbs. cooking oil	salt and pepper
2 chickens cut in serving pieces	2 cups tomato sauce (red or green)

Sprinkle chicken with salt and pepper. Brown in hot oil, then pour over sauce. Simmer until tender (about 45 minutes).

ROASTED CHICKEN

This is sold along most of Mexico's streets and is popular for picnics. I like it even better made at home in the oven with gravy.

1 large chicken	½ cup melted margarine (or
2 cloves garlic mashed	cooking oil)
½ tsp. salt	¼ tsp. pepper

Combine margarine, garlic, salt, and pepper. Heat oven to 350 F. Place chicken in a roasting pan and bake, basting every 10 minutes with margarine mixture until tender. About 1 hour. For gravy, place pan on top of stove with the burner on high. Remove the chicken and add ½ cup water and mix drippings.

TAMALES

These are marvelous! They freeze well.
For: 50 tamales.

Tamales are steamed. If you haven't a steamer, either use a baby bottle sterilizer or place extra corn husks in the bottom of a large pot, add 1 inch hot water in the bottom, being sure tamales *do not* touch water.

For dough:

1 cup vegetable shortening	1 tsp. salt
1 lb. (500 gr.) tamale flour	2 cups consomme
1 Tbs. baking power	

For filling:

1 large chicken boiled and chopped (or 1½ lbs. pork)	2 cups sauce (either Red or Green Tomato or Mole)
50 dried corn husks (soaked over night and drained)	

Beat shortening and salt until fluffy; add tamale flour and consomme and beat until a small ball of dough floats in a glass of water. Add baking powder and beat 5 minutes more. Mix chicken and sauce for filling. Place a spoonful of dough on each husk. Make crevice with spoon and place filling in it. Close loosely (the dough expands when cooked) and fold. Place tamales standing vertically in steaming pot for 1 hour.

TAMALE PIE

Tamales split lengthwise	Chicken, cooked and shredded or chopped
Tomato sauce (red or green) or Mole Sauce	Grated cheese

Grease an ovenproof dish and make layers of all the ingredients in the order given, ending with cheese. Heat in a hot oven 20 minutes or until the cheese melts.

TINGA POBLANA

1 chicken, cut in serving pieces
3 Tbs. cooking oil
½ cup chopped onion
2 cloves garlic, chopped
1-3 chiles Chipotles en Adobo
1 head lettuce

salt and pepper
2 cups chopped tomatoes (or ½ cup canned tomato puree)
2 Tbs. parsley, chopped
3 avocados, sliced

Sprinkle chicken with salt and pepper and brown with onion and garlic in oil. Add tomato and parsley and cook until almost done. Add chiles and finish cooking. To serve: place on a bed of lettuce and cover with avocado slices.

CHICKEN WITH BACON

1 chicken
½ tsp. salt
½ cup water

8 slices bacon
¼ tsp. pepper

Rub salt and pepper on the inside of chicken. Wrap with bacon and roast at 350 F until tender (About 1 hour).

For gravy: Place pan on top of stove with the burner on high. Remove the chicken and add water to drippings. If too greasy, skim with spoon.

BRAINS WITH GREEN SAUCE
(Serves 6 to 8)

2 sets of brains
1 egg (beaten with 1 Tbs. milk)
Cooking oil

salt and pepper
Fine bread crumbs
Green Sauce (see *Index*)

Rinse brains in cold tap water removing any membranes. Dry. Season with salt and pepper, dip in egg, then bread crumbs. Fry until golden in hot oil and serve with Green Sauce.

CHIRUSA

2 onions, sliced
1 tsp. Maggi Sauce
2 Tbs. cooking oil
6 eggs, fried

1-2 green chiles serranos, chopped
1 tsp. Worcestershire Sauce
6 paper-thin sirloin steaks

51

Fry onion and chiles until limp in hot oil. Season with Maggi and Worcestershire Sauce and reserve. Sprinkle steaks with salt and fry. Place on plate followed with fried eggs, then on top the cooked sauce.

GARLIC MEAT LOAF
(Serves 6 to 8)

1 slice white bread	½ cup milk
2 lbs. ground beef	3 large cloves garlic, mashed
2 beef cubes, crushed	½ tsp. pepper
1 egg	1 Tbs. Maggi
1 Tbs. Worcestershire Sauce	6 slices bacon
flour	

Soak bread in milk, then squeeze. Mix bread with everything except flour and bacon. Form a long meat loaf, dredge in flour, then wrap with bacon. Bake at 450 F for 30-40 minutes. Serve hot or cold.

Variations for Meat Loaf:

1. Use only 1 clove garlic and roll prepared meat with hard boiled eggs and/or olives in the center.

2. Serve with tomato sauce.

3. Serve cold with vinaigrette dressing.

GUISADO (Stew)

2 lbs. stew meat beaf, pork or veal	2 Tbs. bacon grease
1 cup chopped onion	1 clove garlic
2 cups chopped tomato (or ½ cup cup canned tomato puree)	1 cup water
	2 Tbs. chopped parsley
½ tsp. salt	¼ tsp. pepper

(For variation: 1 Tbs. chopped pickled chiles or green pepper or chiles poblanos)

Brown meat in bacon grease; add rest of ingredients. Cook in a pressure cooker 1 hour or in a dutch oven, adding 2 more cups of water, about 2 hours, until meat is tender.

HAMBURGUESA (Hamburgers)

Good with pan fried onions.

1½ lbs. ground meat
1 egg
1 Tbs. wine vinegar
½ tsp. salt

½ cup chopped tomato
1 Tbs. chopped onion
1 Tbs. Worcestershire Sauce
¼ tsp. pepper

Combine all ingredients and form patties. Fry, broil, or barbeque.

ALBONDIGAS (Meat Balls)

1½ lbs. ground meat
½ tsp. salt
1/8 tsp. cinnamon
2 cups tomato sauce

1 egg
¼ tsp. pepper
2 hard-boiled eggs
2 leaves fresh mint (optional)

Mix meat with salt, pepper, cinnamon, and raw egg. Cut each hard-boiled egg in small pieces leaving the yolk and white together which are to be used for the center of each meat ball. Heat sauce until it simmers and add one by one each meat ball (adding mint leaves). Simmer until meat is cooked (about 30 minutes). Serve with white rice.

MEAT FRITTERS

Good for leftovers.

2 cups cooked stew meat,
 shredded or chopped
tomato sauce

2 eggs well beaten
cooking oil

Mix meat with eggs and drop by spoonfuls into hot oil. Drain. Heat fritters in tomato sauce to serve.

MILANESAS (Breaded Veal)

When this is served with a fried egg on top it is called "montada" (mounted).

6 veal scallops, pounded paper
 thin
fine bread crumbs
6 fried eggs (optional)

salt and pepper
1 egg well beaten
cooking oil

53

Sprinkle scallops with salt and pepper. Dip in egg, then in bread crumbs and fry until golden in ¼ inch hot cooking oil.

PICADILLO
(Serves 8)

2 lbs. ground meat (beef, pork, or veal)
2 Tbs. bacon grease (or oil)
1 large potato, cooked, and chopped
¼ cup raisins (optional)
¼ cup almonds, chopped (optional)

½ onion, chopped
1 clove garlic, chopped
2 tomatoes, peeled (or ½ cup canned tomato puree)
salt (or beef concentrate) and pepper

Fry meat with onion and garlic in bacon grease until almost cooked. Chop tomatoes (or grind with a little water in blender) and add with the rest of the ingredients to meat. Season to taste and cook until meat is done.

STEAK TIPS MEXICAN STYLE

1½ lbs. tenderloin tips (or sirloin steak) cut in bite-sized pieces
1 Recipe Red Chile Sauce

salt and pepper
2 Tbs. oil

Sprinkle meat with salt and pepper. Stirring constantly sear meat in hot oil. Add sauce and continue cooking until desired doneness. Serve with white rice and refried beans.

CARNE ASADA

Have your butcher cut a beef tenderloin in 3 inch lengths then unroll it (or cut it thin and pound it) into long strips 6 to 8 inches long.
Season meat with salt and lemon juice and fry on a hot griddle (or pan) in the least amount of oil possible.

CARNE ASADA TAMES

Carne Asada served with Broiled Bananas *(See Index)*

54

CARNE ASADA TAMPIQUEÑA

Carne Asada served with Guacamole Sauce, Refried Beans, and an Enchilada de Mole. *(See Index)* This is the "Special Mexican Plate" served to most tourists.

FILETE JACKIE

2 lbs. beef tenderloin	salt and pepper
2 Tbs. butter	2 Tbs. oil
1 Tbs. chopped onion	2 Tbs. flour
2 cups consomee	5 green tomatoes, boiled until soft
½ Chile Chipotle en Adobo (more if you like)	½ tsp. Maggi Sauce

Sprinkle meat with salt and pepper. Brown on all sides in hot butter and oil. Place in a baking dish and bake at 350 F (medium oven) for 25 minutes. Slice and serve with the following sauce.

In butter from meat add onions and flour; let brown. Stirring constantly add consomee, green tomatoes, and Chiles that have been ground in blender. Add Maggi Sauce, and salt and pepper to taste. Strain to serve.

Meat may be browned (and sauce prepared) in advance, then heated in oven to serve.

ROPA VIEJA (Old Clothes)

This goes especially well with flour tortillas.

2 lbs. of beef rump or flank	1 onion
1 clove garlic	½ tsp. salt
¼ tsp. pepper	

Sauce:

2 cups tomato sauce	1 bay leaf
¼ tsp. oregano	½ cup green olives
2 tsp. capers (optional)	

Barely cover meat with water. Add onion and garlic; cook 1 hour in pressure cooker or 2 hours in a large pot. Remove from pot; when cool pull apart in long strips. In a large frying pan combine tomato sauce (or make it), the rest of the ingredients, and meat. Cook together to season 20 minutes.

Any leftovers may be scrambled with eggs for breakfast.

BACKWARDS PORK

I had this at a party and have enjoyed it ever since. I use fresh Apple Sauce (look under *Desserts* in the Index) and either make the following recipe or use leftovers.

1½ lbs. pork loin   salt and pepper to taste
2 cups Apple Sauce

Sprinkle pork with salt and pepper; bake 1 hour at 350 F or until well done. Chill and slice as thin as possible. Serve meat cold with hot apple sauce. If using canned apple sauce sprinkle with cinnamon.

CARNITAS (Fried Pork)

This sets any Mexican's mouth watering.

2 lbs. pork shoulder, cut in bite-   deep fat
   sized pieces   tortillas
any Mexican sauce (Guacamole,
   Chile, etc)

Pork pieces are fried in deep fat until golden and well done. Have tortillas hot for taco making.

PORK ROLL

1½ lbs. pork tenderloin   2 hard-boiled eggs, chopped
¼ cup red pimentos, chopped   ¼ cup parsley, chopped
2 Tbs. bacon grease (or oil)   2 cups tomato sauce (or 1 cup
salt and pepper   water plus 1 cup white wine)

Have butcher open pork and pound flat. Make strips of egg, parsley, and pimento on meat; roll and tie. Sprinkle with salt and pepper; brown in bacon grease; add sauce and cook on medium heat 1 hour until pork is well done.

PORK WITH ADOBO

Adobo is a special blend of peppers and spices. The prepared concentrate is easy and good. The sauce is highly seasoned but not too hot.

Adobo concentrate   pork chops, loin or leg
white vinegar   consomme (optional)

56

Make a runny paste with the adobo and vinegar. Spread over pork and let marinate 6 hours or overnight. Bake at 350 F until meat is well done. If sauce is too tart or hot, add consomme.

PORK WITH ACHIOTE

Achiote is a blend of spices from Yucatan. It is pungent but is not hot.

1½ lbs. pork shoulder, cubed
  (or chops)
½ onion chopped
aluminium foil

1 Tbs. Achiote concentrate
1 orange squeezed (or vinegar)
salt and pepper

Mix achiote with orange juice to make a paste. Place meat on aluminium foil, sprinkle with salt and pepper, then rub with prepared paste. Place onion on top, close foil and bake at 350 F for 1 hour or until meat is tender.

PORK WITH BEER

1½ lbs. pork loin
salt and pepper

2 cups beer

Sprinkle pork with salt and pepper. Bake at 350 F for 1 hour or until well done, basting with beer every 15 minutes.

PORK WITH GREEN PEPPERS OR CHILES POLBANOS

1½ lbs. pork chops, loin or
  shoulder
1 clove garlic, chopped
2 green peppers or chiles pablanos
  skinned, deveined and cut in
  strips

2 Tbs. bacon grease
1 onion, sliced
2 cups tomato chopped (or ½ cup
  canned tomato puree)
salt and pepper

Sprinkle meat with salt and pepper and brown with onion and garlic in hot bacon grease. Add the rest of ingredients and cook until meat is well done. Season to taste with salt and pepper.

PORK WITH GREEN TOMATOES

6-8 pork chops
1 onion, sliced
1 green chile serrano (optional)

2 Tbs. oil
1 clove garlic, chopped
6 green tomatoes, cleaned and cut in fourths

Sprinkle chops with salt and pepper, then brown on both sides with oil. Add green tomatoes, onion, (chile-optional), and garlic. Cook until pork is well done.

PORK WITH JELLY AND RUM

1½ lbs. pork loin
apricot jelly

salt and pepper
rum

Sprinkle pork with salt and pepper; add enough rum to jelly to make liquid. Spread on meat and bake for 1 hour at 350 F or until well done.

PORK WITH ORANGE JUICE

1½ lbs. pork loin
1 cup orange juice
2 Tbs. brown sugar

salt and pepper
1 cup white wine

Sprinkle pork with salt and pepper. Bake at 350 F for 1 hour or until well done, basting with orange juice and wine with sugar every 15 minutes.

PORK ROLL WITH HAM

2 lbs. pork loin, opened flat
1 tsp. granulated chicken concentrate (or 2 cubes crushed)

3-5 slices ham
aluminum foil

Lay opened pork on foil. Sprinkle with chicken concentrate, then cover with ham. Roll, then close foil. Bake at 350 F for 1 hour or until well done.

PORK CHOPS WITH CREAM

6-8 pork chops
½ cup water
1 Tbs. Worcestershire Sauce

salt and pepper
½ cup sweet cream

Sprinkle chops with salt and pepper. Fry until just barely done. Drain off any extra grease. Add water and mix with drippings until they are all unstuck from pan. Add cream and Worcestershire Sauce; let cook down 2 minutes more.

CAMPECHANA COCKTAIL

Oysters and cooked shelled shrimp are placed in shrimp cocktail glasses. They are accompanied with catsup sauce and a plate of the following garnishes:

Parsley-chopped
onion-chopped
lemon slices

avocado-chopped
green chiles serranos-chopped
salt and pepper

CEVICHE

Don't tell anyone the fish is cooked in lemon juice until they try it. Serves 8.

1 lb. white fish fillets cut in bite-
    sized pieces, or shelled shrimp
2 onions, chopped
juice of 1 orange
¼ to ½ cup olive oil
3 Tbs. catsup
½ tsp. Worcestershire Sauce
½ tsp. Tabasco Sauce (or chopped
    green chiles serranos)

½ cup lemon juice
3 large tomatoes, chopped
2 avocados, chopped
½ cup green olives
1 tsp. oregano
3 Tbs. tomato sauce (or tomato
    puree)

Cover fish with lemon juice and let marinate at least 6 hours or overnight. Fish is no longer transparent when cooked. Then add the rest of the ingredients and mix well. Serve in shrimp cocktail cups.

GOUDA CHEESE WITH SEAFOOD

Hollow out the center of a large gouda cheese. Serve filled with shrimp and oysters in White (or cream) sauce.

FISH VERACRUZ STYLE

This is marvelous!

2 lbs. red snapper (or any
  white fish)
¼ onion
2 Tbs. parsley
½ tsp. salt
½ cup green olives
2-4 Tbs. pickled chiles jalapeños

3 large tomatoes
½ cup water
1 clove garlic
4 Tbs. olive oil
¼ tsp. pepper
2 Tbs. capers

Grind tomatoes, onion, garlic, and parsley with water in blender. Strain. Heat olive oil in a roasting pan on top of the stove and add tomato mixture. Lower heat; add fish and rest of ingredients. Baste occasionally until fish is done. About 30 minutes.

FISH WITH MUSTARD

2 lbs. red snapper (or any
  white fish)
2 Tbs. yellow mustard
1 onion, sliced

salt and pepper
4 Tbs. soft butter
1 tomato, sliced
2 Tbs. lemon juice

Sprinkle fish with salt and pepper. Spread with butter and mustard. Place tomato and onion slices on top and sprinkle with lemon juice. Bake in a greased ovenproof dish 30 minutes at 350 F or until fish is flaky.

RED SNAPPER WITH BUTTER

2 lbs. red snapper (or any
  white fish)
¼ cup butter
1 cup water (or white wine)

1 bay leaf
salt and pepper
½ cup parsley, chopped

Rinse fish well and place bay leaf in its stomach. Place in a greased ovenproof dish. Sprinkle with salt and pepper. Dot with butter. Sprinkle with parsley and pour water in bottom of dish. Bake at 350 F basting every 10 minutes or until fish is flaky.

SHRIMP BREAD PUDDING
(A no-fail souffle)

1 lb. shrimp, cooked and peeled
½ cup soft butter
3 eggs, beaten
¼ tsp. each of salt, pepper, and
   paprika

10 slices bread, without crust
2 cups grated cheese
2 cups milk

Spread bread with butter and cut in squares. Grease in ovenproof dish with butter and make layers of bread, shrimp and cheese. Beat milk, eggs, salt, pepper, and paprika; pour over bread. Let sit ½ hour, then bake at 350 F for 45 minutes or until golden.

RED TUNA FISH PIE

1 large can tuna fish
¼ cup olives (green or black)
1 recipe pie crust for a double pie
   (or puff pastry)

2 cups tomato sauce
1 Tbs. capers
1 egg white

Mix tuna, tomato sauce, olives, and capers. Line a large pie plate with ½ pie dough. Fill with tuna mixture, then cover with rest of dough. Spread with egg white (to glaze); make slits with a sharp knife, then bake at 350 F until golden about 30 minutes.

BACALAO (Cod)

Traditional for Christmas this a treat anytime. Remember fish is salted in drying process.

1 lb. dried (salted) cod
1 onion
2 cloves garlic
1 Tbs. fine bread crumbs
1/8 tsp. cinnamon
5 sprigs parsley
1 Tbs. capers
1 cup water
pepper to taste

4 large tomatoes (or 1 cup canned
   tomato puree)
½ cup olive oil
2 cloves
1 Tbs. vinegar
12 green olives
12-16 new (little) potatoes, boiled
   and skinned
1 can chiles jalapeños, or chiles
   güeros

Cover cod with cold tap water and soak 24 hours. The next day rinse 3 times; remove skin and bones. Cut in 1 inch squares.

Toast tomatoes on a hot griddle turning over and over until easy to skin. Grind them in blender with onion and garlic, then strain.

Heat olive oil in a large skillet. Fry bread crumbs, then add tomato mixture, cloves, cinnamon, vinegar, and parsley. Cook down stirring once in a while until tomato separates from oil and sauce is very thick.

Add cod, olives, capers, and water. Lower heat and stir the least amount possible. When fish is done (flaky) season with pepper. To serve: place 2 canned chiles on top and pass the rest.

Vegetables

FRIED ARTICHOKES

6 small artichokes, boiled
1 cup fine bread crumbs
2 eggs, well beaten

1 cup grated cheese (Swiss or
   parmesan)
cooking oil

Stuff cheese between leaves of the artichokes. Dip in egg, then bread crumbs twice. Fry in hot cooking oil (or deep fat) until golden. Drain and serve. May be reheated in oven.

BANANA FRITTERS WITH CHEESE

These go well with pork and are used instead of vegetables.

6 ripe bananas
1-2 eggs separated
flour
cooking oil

12 thin slices cheese
¼ tsp. salt
toothpicks

Cut bananas in half, then lengthwise. Place cheese slice between each half, sandwich style, and spear with toothpicks to hold. Beat egg whites with salt until stiff, then using the same beater add yolks. Dredge bananas with flour, dip in egg mixture, and fry until golden in hot oil. Remove toothpicks. These may be reheated in oven to serve.

BEANS

3 cups any beans
1 Tbs. cooking oil
salt

½ onion
½ lb. pork, bacon, or pickled pork,
   (optional)

Rinse beans in a large pot and cover with water, removing those that float to the top. Soak over night. The next day add onion, oil, (and pork); cook 3 hours (sometimes it takes more depending how fresh beans are) adding *hot* water by cupfuls when beans seem dry. Add salt when beans are cooked.

REFRIED BEANS

3 Tbs. bacon grease
1 clove garlic, chopped
2 cups cooked beans
¼ cup tomato, chopped
   (optional)

4 Tbs. onion chopped
2 inches chorizo, or pork sausage
   (optional)
½ tsp. salt

Saute onion, garlic, and (chorizo-optional) in hot bacon grease until limp. Add beans, salt, and (tomato-optional); while this cooks mash with a potato masher until smooth. Continue cooking until this forms a roll. Don't worry about the crust that forms on the pan because it will lift off.

Serve with Totopos (fried tortillas) and cheese on top; or use for spreading.

SPECIAL REFRIED BEANS

Before frying beans grind them with ½ chile chipotle en adobo in the blender. Then follow the recipe for refried beans.

CHILES POLBANOS AND GREEN BELL PEPPERS

Chiles poblanos are large, dark green, shiny peppers which are used for stuffing, in strips, or in sauces. They are found fresh in some United States cities (or prepared in cans) but may be substituted with green bell peppers which have been skinned and deveined in the same manner as chiles poblanos.

Toast peppers (or chiles) on a hot griddle turning over constantly until soft. Place inside a plastic bag and allow to sweat 10 minutes. Remove from bag, peel off skin and rinse. Soak 30 minutes in salt water. Cut open one one side and remove seeds and veins. Rinse again.

These strips may now be used raw.

Thin strips may be sauteed with onions in oil.

Common stuffings when served cold:

Tuna fish salad	Sardine salad with ½ cup cooked peas

Common stuffings when served hot accompanied with tomato sauce:

Cheese	Refried beans
Rice	Picadillo

CHILES RELLENOS (Stuffed Peppers)

To serve chiles hot, prepare them in the following way:

6-8 chiles poblanos, deveined and skinned	2 cups stuffing (Picadillo, cheese, etc.)
½ cup flour	2 eggs (separated, beat whites stiff, then add yolks)
cooking oil	
toothpicks	tomato sauce

Stuff chiles with filling and carefully close with toothpicks. Roll them in flour, dip in egg, and fry in hot oil until golden. Drain and remove toothpicks. Reheat in a hot oven in tomato sauce.

CORN FRITTERS

1 can corn   1 cup flour
1 tsp. baking power   3 eggs, well beaten
¼ tsp. salt

Add in the order given and mix well. Drop by spoonfuls into deep fat and cook until golden. Drain on paper towels and serve hot.

CORN ON THE COB

This is sold on street corners.

Pour over each ear of cooked corn on the cob:

salt   sweet cream
parmesan cheese

Serve with Tabasco Sauce or cayenne pepper for those who like "chile"; paprika for those who don't.

CORN PUDDING

Good served with meat and gravy or honey.

4 ears corn, degrained (6 if ears   1 cup milk
   are small)   ½ cup butter, melted (or margarine)
1 cup flour   1 tsp. baking powder
½ tsp. salt   2 eggs, separated

Grind corn with milk in blender. Pour into an ovenproof dish and mix with flour, baking powder, and salt. Beat egg whites until stiff then add yolks. Gently fold this into corn. Bake at 350 F for 30 minutes or until golden on top.

FRESH CORN TAMALES

6 ears fresh corn   milk
½-1 cup grated cheese   ½ tsp. salt

Peel corn but reserve husks. Degrain corn and grind in blender with the least amount of milk possible. Use cheese to thicken and add salt. Using the largest husks place 1 Tbs. mixture in the center of each. Fold sides first then ends. In a large pot place the rest of the husks and add 1 to 2 inches hot water. Water should not cover husks. Stand the tamales on this base, cover pot, and steam 15 minutes or until corn mixture no longer sticks to the husks.

GARBANZOS (Chickpeas)

4-6 slices bacon, chopped   2 chorizos, chopped (or pork
½ cup onion, chopped   sausages)
1½ cups tomato, chopped   4 cups chickpeas, cooked
4 cups spinach, cooked and   salt
   chopped

Saute onion with bacon and chorizos until limp. Add tomato and cook 5 minutes. Add chickpeas and spinach. Continue to cook until mixture is thick. Add salt to taste.

LENTILS
(Serves 6 to 8)

4-6 slices bacon, chopped   ½ cup onion, chopped
1½ cups tomato, chopped   4 cups lentils, cooked
salt

Saute onion with bacon until limp. Add tomatoes and cook down 5 minutes. Add lentils and continue cooking until mixture is thick. Add salt to taste.

MUSHROOM FILLING FOR CREPES

1 lb. fresh mushrooms, washed   ¼ cup flour
   and well drained   1 cup sweet cream
½ tsp. salt   ¼ tsp. white pepper

Place mushrooms in a heavy skillet *(no oil)* and cook on low heat until they let out their water. Sprinkle over flour, add the rest of ingredients. Stir constantly until flour no longer tastes raw (about 4 minutes) and use for filling crepes.

NOPALES OR SNAP BEANS

Nopales are the tender leaves of a prickley pear cactus. Cooked snap beans may be used in any recipe calling for cooked nopales.
To prepare fresh nopales:

2 cups nopales, chopped (5 large leaves)

½ onion
½ tsp. salt

Remove all stickers with a sharp knife and rinse in cold water. Chop, then boil with salt and onion in water until easily pierced with a fork. Rinse again in cold water and drain.

NOPALES OR SNAP BEANS WITH BACON

4 cups nopales or snap beans, cooked
½ cup tomato, chopped

2 strips bacon, chopped
2 Tbs. onion, chopped
½ tsp. salt

Fry bacon until crisp, add onion and tomato, cook until mushy. Add nopales or snap beans and cook 10 minutes more.

POTATO FRITTERS

1 lb. potatoes (2 or 3 large)
½ tsp. salt
½ cup grated cheese

¼ cup milk
1 egg beaten
hot oil

Boil potatoes in salt water. Remove skins and mash with milk, salt, cheese, and egg. Shape into patties and fry in oil until golden.
Optional: 1 fried mashed chorizo may be added after egg.

POTATOES DEVILED

3 large baked potatoes
¼ cup butter
salt and pepper to taste

4 Tbs. deviled ham
¼ cup sweet cream

Split potatoes lengthwise and remove pulp. Mash pulp with deviled ham, butter, cream, and season with salt and pepper. Fill shells and heat in a hot oven 20 minutes.

VEGETABLE PEARS STUFFED

3 cooked vegetable pears
3 Tbs. canned tomato puree
  (or tomato sauce)
6 Tbs. parmesan cheese

3 slices bacon, chopped
salt and pepper to taste
6 Tbs. fine bread crumbs
olive oil

Split vegetable pears lengthwise, discard pits, and remove pulp being careful not to break shells. Fry bacon until crisp, add tomato and pulp. Mash and season with salt and pepper, letting it all cook together 5 minutes. Fill shells. Sprinkle bread crumbs mixed with cheese on top and place in an ovenproof dish with 1/8 inch water. Heat in a hot oven 20 minutes or until the tops are brown.

VEGETABLE PEARS WITH BUTTER AND CREAM

3 vegetable pears, cooked
6 Tbs. cream

6 Tbs. butter

Heat cooked, skinned, chopped vegetable pears in butter and pour over cream to serve. Or cut lengthwise, mash pulp with butter and cream; stuff shells and heat in oven.

ZUCCHINI AND CORN

¼ cup chopped onion
4 cups chopped zucchini
1 tomato, chopped

4 Tbs. bacon grease
1 ear corn degrained
salt and pepper to taste

Fry onion in bacon grease until limp. Add rest of the ingredients and simmer until zucchini is tender. (20-30 minutes).

Salads
and
Cold Dishes

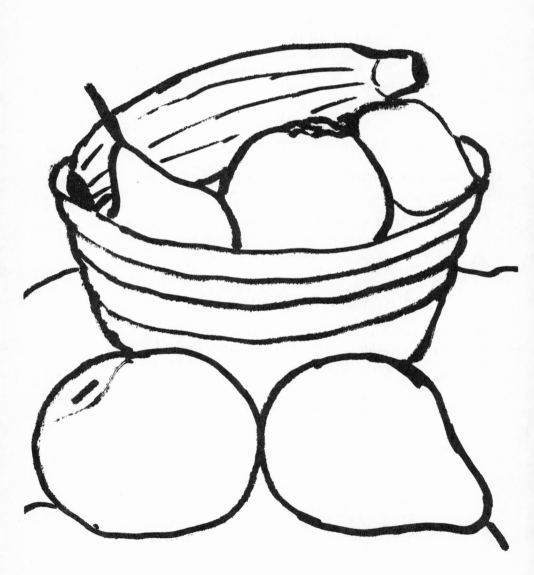

AVOCADO AND SHRIMP SALAD

Good for a first course or a light meal.

1 lb. shrimp, cooked, peeled, and chopped
2 Tbs. parsley, chopped
1 green chile serano, chopped (or Tabasco Sauce)
lettuce

2 tomatoes, chopped
½ onion, chopped
2 Tbs. corriander, chopped
Mustard Salad Dressing (see page 75)

Mix all ingredients together and place on lettuce to serve.

AVOCADO COCKTAIL

Shrimp cocktail glasses filled with sliced avocado.

Garnish: catsup and chopped: onion, green chiles serranos, parsley, corriander, and lemon slices.

STUFFED AVOCADOS

Split avocados in half, remove pits, and lay on lettuce. Stuff with one of the following.

canned eels
tuna fish salad
shrimp salad

sardine salad
chicken salad

AVOCADO SALAD DRESSING

1 cup French dressing

1 ripe avocado

Mash avocado in the bottom of salad bowl. Stirring constantly add French dressing.

73

ESCABECHE FOR SHRIMP OR FISH (Marinade)

2 lbs. shrimp, boiled and peeled (or 2 lbs. fish slices, dipped flour and fried in oil)
1 onion sliced
1 tsp. salt
1 tsp. pepper (or whole black peppers)
1 sliced lemon
1 cup red wine vinegar
2/3 cup canned red pimentos
1 cup carrots, sliced and parboiled 10 minutes
1 cup olive oil
4 cloves garlic
1 tsp. oregano
1 bay leaf
3 cloves
(1 small can chiles serranos, or jalapeños en escabeche)
2/3 cup green olives with pimentos

Saute onion and garlic in olive oil until limp, add shrimp, carrots, and rest of the ingredients. When it boils remove from heat, cool, then refrigerate. If the sauce is too sour, water may be added to taste.

ESCABECHE FOR MEAT OR CHICKEN

Follow the recipe for Escabeche for Shrimp, substituting 2 lbs. meat or chicken instead of shrimp.

ESCABECHE FOR VEGETABLES

Follow the recipe for Escabeche for Shrimp. Subsitute 2 lbs. mixed vegetables (cauliflower, snap beans, potatoes) parboiled 10 minutes instead of shrimp.

CHILES EN NOGADA

8 chiles poblanos, skinned and deveined (see page 66)
1/8 tsp. cloves
¼ cup acitron, chopped (optional)
2 granadas, peeled and seeds separated
1 recipe Picadillo, with apples instead of potatoes
1/8 tsp. cinnamon
1½ cups Nut Sauce (made with walnuts when in season)

Mix picadillo with cloves, cinnamon, and acitron (optional). Stuff peppers, spread sauce on top, and decorate with granada seeds. Serve cold.

NOPAL SALAD

This may be made early and keeps well in the refrigerator.

2 cups cooked nopales (or snap beans) chopped
4 Tbs. cottage cheese
2 Tbs. vinegar
¼ tsp. pepper

4 Tbs. onion, chopped
2 tomatoes; 1 chopped, 1 sliced
6 Tbs. salad oil
½ tsp. salt

Combine nopales, onion, chopped tomato, and cottage cheese. Mix oil, vinegar, salt and pepper (or any good French dressing), and pour over salad. Decorate with sliced tomato.

POTATO SALAD WITH MUSTARD DRESSING

1 clove garlic, mashed
½ tsp. yellow mustard
2 lemons
¼ tsp. pepper
4 large potatoes, cooked, skinned and cubed

½ tsp. salt
½ cup salad oil
few drops of Worcestershire Sauce
1 large sliced onion
½ cup watercress chopped (optional)

Prepare dressing by combining all ingredients except for potatoes, onions, and watercress in a covered glass jar and shaking until well mixed. Pour over onion and let marinate ½ hour. Add potatoes and watercress (optional) and serve.

RADISH SALAD

radishes, sliced
corriander, chopped
tomato, chopped
French dressing

parsley, chopped
watercresss, chopped
cottage cheese

This can be put together in any proportion, but cottage cheese is always crumbled on top.

SALPICON

A meat salad served as a main course.

2 lbs. beef rump or flank
1 clove garlic
¼ tsp. pepper
½ onion, chopped
1 cucumber, sliced

1 onion
½ tsp. salt
2 tomatoes, 1 chopped and 1 sliced
1 avocado, sliced
1 cup French dressing

Barely cover meat and onion with water. Add salt, pepper, and garlic. Cook 1 hour in pressure cooker (2 hours on stove) until tender. Remove meat and shred in long strips (or strings).

Mix meat, chopped tomato, and onion. Decorate top of salad with cucumber, avocado, and sliced tomato; pour over dressing.

SPINACH AND WATERCRESS SALAD

5 cups fresh spinach, chopped
6 slices salami, chopped

1 cup watercress, chopped
½ cup French dressing (I use 3 parts oil to 1 part vinegar)

Combine everything and serve.

TUNA FISH SALAD

A change from the tuna-mayonaise circuit.

1 large can tuna fish, drained
¼ cup onion, chopped
1 cup lettuce, chopped
2 Tbs. vinegar

½ cup tomato, chopped
2 stalks celery and leaves, chopped
4 Tbs. cottage cheese
1 Tbs. oil

Toss everything together and serve as salad or hors d'oeuvre on toast.

RED CABBAGE SALAD

1 small head red cabbage, shredded
1 tsp. oregano

¼ cup oil
2 lemons

Mix cabbage with oil, sqeeze over lemon, and add oregano.

Beverages

ATOLE

Traditionally eaten with tamales, Atole has the consistency of a runny cornstarch pudding.

½ cup cornstarch
4 cups milk
2 cups water
3/4 cup sugar

1 cup fresh fruit, ground and strained (or canned fruit or marmalade)

Dissolve cornstarch in water. Heat milk. When it boils add cornstarch little by little, stirring constantly. Let boil 3 minutes, then add fruit (if using canned or marmalade use less sugar) and sugar. Serve hot.

For plain atole: add 1 cup milk (or water) instead of fruit and 1 stick cinnamon.

CAFÉ DE OLLA (Mexican Coffee)

Genuine cafe de olla is coffee and water boiled in a large clay pot with cinnamon and brown sugar. My objection is that you always receive coffee grounds in your cup. Here is a better and easier way:

Make regular coffee in your normal way. To serve: Boil 15 minutes with cinnamon and brown sugar. Calculate for each 2 cups: 1 stick cinnamon and 2 tsp. brown sugar.

FRESH FRUIT DRINKS

For lunch or hot days special beverages are made out of fresh fruit. These are seldom measured as the fruit varies in size and sweetness. Frozen fruit may be used but remember that it is already sweetened.

Lemonade: Grind in the blender the rind of 1 lemon with a little water and add to lemonade (lemon juice, water or soda water, and sugar).

Pineapple-ade: Peel a fresh pineapple and puree chunks in the blender with water. Strain into a large pitcher and add enough water to make drinkable. Sweeten to taste.

Other Flavors: Instead of Pineapple, substitute melon, peaches, mangos, strawberries, or watermelon.

SANGRÍA

Sangría is lemonade with an equal amount of red wine poured on top but not mixed. This is especially pretty for a party prepared in a crystal pitcher or punch bowl with thin slices of lemon floating in it.

79

HOT CHOCOLATE

4 cups milk   6 oz. sweet dark chocolate
¼ tsp. cinnamon   1 egg (optional)

Heat everything until chocolate melts. To serve: twirl a wire wisp between hands until chocolate is frothy. (To add egg: whiz in blender with a little hot chocolate then add to rest.)

JAMAICA

1½ cups Jamaica flowers   3 qts. (12 cups) water
sugar to taste

Rinse then boil Jamaica 10 to 15 minutes until water is dark red. Strain, then add sugar to taste. Serve cold. Or boil jamaica in 4 cups water; strain, then add rest of water to this concentrate.

KALUA

A coffee liquor. Serving variations:

drink plain   mix equal amounts Kaula and sweet
pour over vanilla ice cream   cream

TEA: LEMON, ORANGE, CINNAMON, MINT

Leaves are added to boiling water and boiled 5 to 10 minutes. Amounts are for 1 cup water. Drink hot or cold.

Lemon—2 fresh or dried leaves   Orange—2 fresh or dried leaves
Cinnamon—1 stick   Mint—2 fresh or dried leaves

TEPACHE

A fermented drink made with fruit peelings. I make it the same day I make fruit salad.

skin of 1 pineapple   skins of 5 bananas
skins of 3-5 oranges   2 cones of piloncillo (or 2 cups
                                brown sugar)

Wash fruit well before peeling. Cover peelings with water in a large glass, enamel or ceramic bowl. Add piloncillo. Cover with a clean kitchen towel and let sit three days at room temperature. Serve cold.

Desserts

ALMOND CUSTARD

3/4 cup almonds, blanched   4 cups milk
4 egg yolks   3/4 cup sugar
1 tsp. vanilla or almond extract   cinnamon (optional)

Grind ½ cup almonds in blender with 1 cup milk. Mix this with rest of milk, egg yolks, and sugar; cook on low heat stirring constantly until thick. Add vanilla or almond extract and pour into serving dish. Decorate with rest of almonds toasted. (Or dust with cinnamon.)

APPLE OR BANANA FRITTERS

My children like this for breakfast.

3 cups apple, grated coarsely, or   3 eggs
  sliced bananas   butter, cinnamon, sugar, cream

Mix fruit with egg and drop by teasponfuls into hot butter. Cook until golden on both sides. Sprinkle with cinnamon and sugar. Serve with a pitcher of cream.

APPLE SAUCE

Make Fruit in Syrup (Apples) on page 82. Mash or grind in blender. Cook down until desired consistency is reached. Serve hot or cold.

SLICED APPLES

6 large tart apples, peeled and   sugar
  sliced   cinnamon
water   4 Tbs. butter

Make layers of apples sprinkling with sugar and cinnamon between each. Add enough water until it comes slightly below the first layer. Slice butter on top. Cover and simmer 15 minutes or until brown and limp.

BANANAS BROILED

Leave skin on bananas; cut lengthwise. Sprinkle with brown sugar and place under broiler until brown. These are served with steak or as a dessert.

BANANAS FRIED

Peel ripe bananas and cut lengthwise. Fry in hot cooking oil until golden, then drain. Sprinkle with sugar and cinnamon to serve.

CAKES WITH WHIPPED CREAM

2 layers yellow cake
2 cups whipping cream
cognac, brandy, or rum
1 cup powdered sugar (more if
   you like things very sweet)

1 cup toasted slivered almonds;
   pine nuts or pecans chopped
   (optional) or 2 cups sliced man-
   goes, (peaches, strawberries, and
   bananas)

Sprinkle layers with cognac. Whip cream until stiff with powdered sugar. To put together, spread cream and sprinkle with nuts or fruit between layers and on top and sides. Serve cold.

CAPIROTADA

Traditionally this recipe uses all of the syrup. I use one-half then serve the rest in a pitcher.

8, 1" slices French bread (fresh
   or stale)
1 cup water
1 stick cinnamon
½ cup pecans (or blanched
   almonds), chopped

cooking oil
1 cup brown sugar (1 cone pillon-
   cillo)
2 cloves
½ cup raisins

Fry French bread in hot oil (like croutons) until golden on both sides, then drain on paper towels. Make syrup with brown sugar, water, cinnamon, and cloves; boil 15 minutes. Place bread in an ovenproof dish and pour over syrup, pecans, and raisins. Heat 15 minutes in the oven at 350 F to serve.

CAJETA

This is a sweet milk dessert which reminds me of carmel sauce. It is eaten plain, on bread, ice cream, or in crepes. It can be bought or made at home in the following way:

Place 1 to 2 cans unopened of condensed milk in the pressure cooker. Fill with water to one-half level of can. Cover pot and cook 20 minutes. Remove can but do not open until cool.

CREPES
(Serves 6)

3 eggs

½ tsp. salt (or 1 tsp. sugar when using for desserts)

1½ cups milk

1 cup flour

butter and waxed paper

Using a wire wisp or in blender mix eggs, milk, salt, and flour to remove any lumps. This should have the consistency of cream.

Quickly pass butter with a piece of waxed paper over pan before making each crepe. (I prefer using a teflon pan, thus skipping greasing).

Using a soup laddle or a large spoon measure dough into pan. Move around to form a thin pancake. Turn over when edges are brown.

CREPES WITH CAJETA

1 recipe of Crepes

1 cup milk

½ cup Cajeta

½ cup chopped pecans

Fold crepes in fourths and place in serving dish. Heat Cajeta with milk and pour over crepes. Sprinkle with pecans and heat 15 minutes to serve. (Cajeta may be used without diluting but is very sweet).

CHURROS

Wonderful on a cold night with hot chocolate or an emergency dessert. The dough is the same as for cream puffs but fried in 4 inch lengths. When dropped by spoonful it is the classic French "pet de nonne".

1 cup hot water

1 cup flour

4 eggs

cooking oil (or deep fat)

½ cup butter (or margarine)

½ tsp. salt

sugar and cinnamon, or powdered sugar

85

Boil butter and salt in water until melted. Add flour. Stirring constantly cook until mixture forms a ball. Remove from heat and add eggs one at a time beating between each addition.

Push dough through a pastry tube with the largest open tip in 4 to 6 inch lengths (or drop by spoonfuls) into hot oil. Fry until golden, then drain. Sprinkle with cinnamon and sugar.

FLAN (Carmel Custard)

2 cups sugar
1 1/3 cup whole milk
1 tsp. vanilla

1 1/3 cup (1 can) condensed milk
3 eggs

To carmelize mold: place sugar in heavy skillet over high heat. Stir constantly until liquid and is light brown. Using pot holders, pour hot sugar into a small ring mold and coat the center and sides. (Be careful, this can cause bad burns.)

Combine milks, eggs, and vanilla. Strain and pour into carmelized mold. Bake at 350 F set in a pan with 1 inch hot water 40 minutes or until a knife comes out clean. When room temperature, turn over on platter.

FRUIT IN SYRUP

6 apples, sliced (peaches or pears)
1 Tbs. lemon juice

¼ to ½ cup sugar
¼ tsp. cinnamon

Barely cover apples with water. Add sugar, lemon juice, and cook until tender about 20 minutes. Serve hot or cold.

GRAPEFRUIT

4 grapefruits
cinnamon

sugar

Peel grapefruit and remove membrane from sections. Place on a platter and sprinkle with sugar and cinnamon. Serve cold.

ICE CREAM

2lbs. fresh peaches, mangos, or
   strawberries

1 1/3 cups (1 can) condensed milk

Skin and pit selected fruit. Grind in blender with condensed milk until smooth. Pour into ice trays and place in freezer.

JERICAYA (Custard With Almonds)

4 cups milk
1 cup sugar
¼ cup almonds, blanched, sliced,
 and toasted

4 eggs
1 tsp. vanilla

Mix milk, eggs, and sugar. Cook until the milk forms a skin. Add vanilla and pour into an ovenproof dish. Bake at 350 F set in a pan with 1 inch hot water 40 minutes or until a knife comes out clean. Sprinkle almonds on top to serve.

LEMON PIE WITH CONDENSED MILK

1 1/3 cups condensed milk (1 can)
grated rind of 1 lemon (or lime)
3 Tbs. sugar
1 baked pie crust (or Graham
 cracker crust)

½ cup lemon juice (or lime juice)
2 eggs, separated
1/8 tsp. salt

Mix condensed milk, lemon juice, lemon rind, and egg yolks; pour into crust. Beat egg whites until stiff with sugar and salt; spread over filling.

Brown egg whites in a hot oven 3 minutes. This can be served room temperature, cold, or frozen.

MANGO DESSERT

A good every day dessert. Place canned mangos or peaches in serving dish. Mix condensed milk with orange juice and pour over fruit. Sprinkle over raisins. Serve cold.

NATILLAS

A creamy cornstarch pudding—this is the best I've eaten anywhere.

2 Tbs. cornstarch
1 1/3 cup condensed milk (1 can)
4 egg yolks
½ cup raisins (optional)

4 cups milk
1 stick cinnamon
cinnamon powder

87

Wet cornstarch in a little milk, then combine with the rest of the milk, condensed milk, and cinnamon stick. Cook on low heat, stirring constantly until pudding begins to thicken. Remove from heat, add egg yolks, stirring between each addition and return to heat, cooking while stirring until it has the consistency of cream sauce. Strain. Refrigerate. To serve: cover top with powdered cinnamon.

OLD CAKE

1 cup flour	1 tsp. baking powder
¼ tsp. salt	6 eggs, separated
3/4 cup sugar	1 can pineapple slices
1 cup whipped cream	Kirsch

Sift flour, salt, and baking powder 6 times. Beat egg yolks with one-half the amount sugar until thick and lemon colored. Beat whites with rest of sugar until stiff. Mix yolks and whites; add flour slowly.

Place in a cake mold that has been greased and floured. Bake 30 minutes at 350 F or until top springs back when touched with finger tips. When cool, remove from pan sprinkle with Kirsch and decorate with whipped cream, pineapple slices.

PUFF PASTE TART

Frozen puff paste (thawed)	1 jar any jam or jelly
egg white	sugar

Roll out 2 long strips of puff paste on a floured board. Place 1 strip on a greased cookie sheet and spread with jam. Cover with the other strip, then cut edges straight and pinch together. Paint with egg white and sprinkle with sugar. Cut top crosswise at 2 inch intervals. Bake at 350 F for 30 minutes or until golden.

PUEBLA SWEET POTATO CANDY

2 cups cooked, mashed, strained sweet potatoes	2 cups sugar
½ tsp. orange, lemon, cherry extract, or cinnamon	1 Tbs. lemon juice
	butter
colored tissue paper squares with fringed edges	sugar (optional)

Cook sweet potatoes with sugar, stirring constantly until mixture does not stick to sides of pot and forms a ball (about 45 minutes). Remove from heat and add extract.

When cool enough to handle, butter hands and make candy cigars 2 to 3 inches long. Leave plain or roll in sugar. Let dry two days on a tray lined with waxed paper in a cool place. Wrap in tissue paper and twist at edges.

SWEET PUMPKIN

Mexicans celebrate the "Day of the Dead", Novemver 2, by visiting dead relatives in the cemetery. Symbolic offerings are left on graves. These vary from region to region. Pan de Muerto (Bread of the Dead) and sugar skulls are purchased in the Valley of Mexico. Sweet pumpkin is traditionally made at home for this holiday.

2 lbs. pumpkin
2 cinnamon sticks
2 oranges, sliced

2 lbs. brown sugar (or piloncillo)
4 whole cloves

Wash pumpkin, remove pulp and seeds, then cut in 4 inch pieces and remove the skin with a sharp knife. Cook pumpkin with rest of ingredients on low heat stirring constantly until tender. Serve at room temperature or cold.

[Pumpkin seeds may be dried in the sun, then baked with salt until crisp and eaten like peanuts.]

ROYAL EGGS
(Serves 10 to 12)

For those who don't like very sweet desserts use only half the amount of sugar and water and add more juice.

9 eggs separated
4 cups sugar
1 cup orange (or pineapple) juice
butter

9 Tbs. rice flour
3 cups water
1/3 to ½ cup rum
½ cup toasted almonds (optional)

Beat egg whites until stiff. Still beating, add rice flour spoon by spoon, then yolks, one at a time. Pour into a 9" x 12" pyrex dish that has been greased with butter. Bake at 500 F for 20 minutes or until a toothpick comes out clean.

While dough is baking make syrup. Heat water and sugar; when it boils, add orange juice and rum. Boil 2 minutes more. Spoon this over cooked dough when it is removed from oven. Cool, refrigerate, and serve with almonds sprinkled on top (optional) the next day.

SHERBERTS

These are very easy, good, and nutritious. A jar of any "fresh fruit drink" is prepared adding more sugar than usual and vegetable color. This is frozen in any kind of ice cream freezer (hand cranked or electric). These don't keep well for over a week but it doesn't matter as it is usually finished off the first day.

TORREJAS

This is traditionally served when the baby of the household has a first tooth.

1 cup milk
8 slices white bread with the crust removed and cut in four (or pound cake, or slices of sweet rolls)
1 stick cinnamon
rum

1 tsp. vanilla
2 eggs, separated
1 cup brown sugar (or 1 cone piloncillo)
1 cup water
4 cloves
deep fat

Boil milk with vanilla until the milk forms a skin. Beat egg whites until stiff, then add yolks. Dip bread in milk, then egg and fry in deep fat. Serve with syrup made with sugar, water, cinnamon, cloves, and a dash of rum. These may be reheated in the oven.

STRAWBERRY JELLO

A quick mousse and very good.

2 cups strawberries
1 large pack strawberry Jello
½ cup cold water
1 can (1 1/3 cup) condensed milk

1 cup boiling water
1 cup whipped cream and extra strawberries for decoration (optional)

90

Grind strawberries with condensed milk in blender. Mix Jello with boiling water; when dissolved add cold water and strawberry mixture. Chill in a 6 cup ring mold 3 hours or until firm. Unmold by dipping mold quickly in a pan of hot water and invert on platter.

ROMPOPE JELLO

Rompope is a thick egg nog bought at the liquor store or super market.

1 large pack peach (or pineapple) Jello
1 cup dried fruit (apricots, prunes etc.)

2½ cups boiling water
1½ cups Rompope

Dissolve Jello in boiling water. Add Rompope and fruit (or line mold with fruit) and chill until firm. Unmold to serve.

ORANGE CUSTARD

1 can (1 1/3 cup) condensed milk
1 Tbs. grated orange rind
1 ring mold coated with carmelized sugar (see Flan)

1 can (1 1/3 cup) orange juice
5 eggs

Mix all ingredients in blender. Pour in mold. Bake at 350 F. Set in a pan with 1 inch hot water 40 minutes or until a knife inserted in center comes out clean.

Turn over on serving platter when warm.

ZAPOTE

A shiny green fruit about the size of a small grapefruit. It is ready to prepare when mushy to squeeze and is used for dessert.

4 zapotes
½ cup sugar

1 orange (2 tangerines)

Wash and peel zapote. Using your largest strainer, strain pulp with orange juice. Add sugar and serve cold.

91

ENGLISH/SPANISH FOR INGREDIENTS

Acitron—acitrón
almonds—almendras
apple—manzana
apricot—chabacano
anchovies—anchoas
artichokes—alcachofas
avocado—aguacate
Bacon—tocino
baking powder—Royal
bananas—plátanos
bay leaf—hoja de laurel
beans—frijoles
beef—rés
brains—sesos
bread—pan
bread crumbs—pan molido
bread, french—pan frances
butter—mantequilla
Cabbage—col
capers—alcaparras
carrots—zanahorias
cauliflower—coliflór
celery—apio
cheese—queso
chicken—pollo
chickpea—garbanzo
chocolate—chocolate
cinnamon—canela
cloves—clavo de olór
coffee—café
consomme—consomé
corn—elote, maíz
corn husks—hojas de elote
corn starch—maizena
coriander—cilantro
cottage cheese—queso cottage,
    queso anejo
crabs—jaibas, cangrejos
cream—crema
cream, sour—crema ácida
crepes—crepas
cucumbers—pepinos

Eels—angulas, anguilas
eggs—huevos
extracts—extractos
Fish—pescado
fish, white—robalo, huachinango
flour—harina
Garlic—ajo
grapefruit—toronja
Ham—jamón
ham, deviled—jamón endiablado
hominy—maiz cacahuatzintle
Ice Cream—helado
Jelly—mermelada
juice—jugo
Leeks—poros
lemon—limón
lemon rind—cáscara de limón
lentils—lentejas
lettuce—lechuga
liver—hígado
Margarine—margarina
meat—carne
milk—leche
milk, evaporated—leche (Clavel)evaporada
milk, condensed—leche (Nestle)condensad:
mint—hierba buena
mushrooms—champignones,
    hongos
mustard—mostaza
Noodles—tallarines
nutmeg—nuez moscada
nuts—nueces
Oil—aceite
oil, olive—aceite de oliva
olives—aceitunas
oranges—naranjas
oregano—orégano
Peas—chícharos
parsley—perejíl
peaches—duraznos
Pecans—nueces
pepper—pimienta

92

pickles—pepinos
pimentos—pimientos
pineapple—piña
pork—puerco
potatoes—papas
puff paste—pasta de hojaldra
pumpkin—calabaza de castilla
Radish—rábano
raisins—pasas
Salt—sal
sardines—sardinas
sauce—salsa
shrimp—camarón
snap beans—ejotes
spaghetti—espagueti
spinach—espinaca
strawberries—fresas
sugar—azúcar
sugar, brown—azúcar moscada-
  vada
sugar, powdered—azúcar glass
sweet potatoes—camotes

Tea—te
tomatoes—jitomatoes, tomates, rojos
tomatoes, green—tomates verdes
tomato, puree—puré de tomate
tissue paper—papel de china
tuna fish—atún
turkey—pavo, guajolote
Vanilla—vainilla
veal—ternera
vegetables—verduras
vegetable pears—chayotes
vegatable shortening—manteca vegetal
  manteca Inca
vermicelli—fidéo
vinegar—vinagre
Water—agua
watercress—berros
watermellon—sandía
wine—vino
wine, red—vino tinto
wine, white—vino blanco
Zucchini—calabacitas

MEASUREMENTS

1 oz.—30 gr.
2 oz.—60 gr.
3 oz.—85 gr.
4 oz.—115 gr.
5 oz.—140 gr.
6 oz.—170 gr.
7 oz.—200 gr.
8 oz. (½ lb.)—225 gr.
10 oz.—280 gr.
16 oz. (1 lb.)—450 gr.

1 tsp.—5 gr.
1 Tbs. (3 tsp.)—15 gr.
2 Tbs. (1 oz.)—30 gr.
4 Tbs.—¼ cup
8 Tbs.—½ cup
16 Tbs.—1 cup

1 Liter—4 cups
1 kilo—2.2 lbs.

Index